A Bustle & Sew Publication

Copyright © Bustle & Sew Limited 2014

The right of Helen Dickson to be identified as the author of this work has been asserted in accordance with the Copyright, Designs and Patents Act 1988.

All rights reserved. No part of this publication may be reproduced, stored in a retrieval system or transmitted in any form, or by any means, without the prior written permission of the author, nor be otherwise circulated in any form of binding or cover other than that in which it is published and without a similar condition being imposed on the subsequent purchaser.

Every effort has been made to ensure that all the information in this book is accurate. However, due to differing conditions, tools and individual skills, the publisher cannot be responsible for any injuries, losses and other damages that may result from the use of the information in this book.

ISBN-13: 978-1503055575
ISBN-10: 1503055574

First published 2014 by:
Bustle & Sew
Coombe Leigh
Chillington
Kingsbridge
Devon TQ7 2LE
UK

www.bustleandsew.com

Welcome ....

Hello again!

I can hardly believe that a whole month has gone by and already it's time to write my introduction to the latest issue of this magazine. But the year is turning, the clocks have gone back and the leaves are falling from the trees. Inside all is warm and cosy, the log burner is alight and it's the perfect time to curl up in your favourite chair to plan your Christmas (yes, it's not too far away now) sewing.

In this month's issue you'll discover the most adorable little reindeer to stitch (at least I think so anyway), as well as a completely revised and updated pattern for an old favourite, the Candy Cone Mouse. This time he is removeable from his cone and will make a delightful pocket toy once all the sweets are eaten.

As usual Rosie has searched the internet to bring you some really Lovely Ideas, as well as interviewing this month's Meet the Maker - Catherine Beaumont of Peonie Cole. Catherine's designs are simply beautiful and I do hope you'll enjoy reading all about her creative process.

Next month is our Christmas issue, with lots of seasonal fun between the covers, as well as our 2015 calendar - can it really be almost 2015!?! It will, as always, be published on the last Thursday of the month, so look out for it on Thursday 27 November.

Until then, lots of love, and happy stitching from us all here at Bustle & Sew HQ.

"I like to keep small magnetic marbles in the dish of straight pins I put out while pinning fabric. That way, if the pins tip (and they often do!) they don't scatter everywhere!"

Many thanks to Ruth for this top tip.

Tip for Stitchers

November

Waste Not, Want Not	Page 39
Poetry Corner: Rich Days	Page 41
November's Favourite Blogs	Page 42
Village Applique Lampshade	Page 43
Transferring your Pattern	Page 46
And finally ….	Page 49
Baking Conversion Tables	Page 50
Templates	Page 51

Contributors

Contents

November Almanac	Page 6
Movember Hoops	Page 7
Feeling Cosy	Page 10
Top Tips for Etsy Selling	Page 12
Christmas Reindeer Softie	Page 13
Simple Crochet Flowers	Page 16
Freestyle & very easy!	Page 17
Friends Forever Hoop Art	Page 21
Stir Up Sunday	Page 23
Blackberry & Apple Loaf Recipe	Page 24
Baking Shopping Corner	Page 26
Embroidered Floral Alphabet	Page 27
Meet the Maker: Peonie Cole	Page 32
Deer Printable	Page 34
Candy Cone Mouse	Page 35
Crochet Fox Basket	Page 38

Rosie Studholme

Puts together all our lovely ideas, shopping and baking pages as well as researching/editing our features and interviews.

Catherine Beaumont

Catherine is the creative force behind Peonie Cole - featured in this month's "Meet the Maker"

Alice from Close Encounters of the Baking Kind

Alice brings us this month's totally delicious recipe for Blackberry & Apple Loaf - yum!

November

In nature, November is the time when autumn fades into winter, when the last leaves fall from the trees and many hibernating animals commence their long winter sleep.

November is the time for a final farewell to the warmer weather and to snuggle down with a good book or some stitching in front of a crackling open fire. Deep reds, warm rich russets and jewel coloured berries make us feel warm, safe and snug from the cold dark days outside. It's time to enjoy the garden from indoors, bringing inside dried hydrangea heads, stems of berries and hips, and beautiful golden leaves to decorate our rooms.

The Anglo-Saxons named November *Blotmonath* or "blood month" or *Windmonath* "wind month" - the former because it was time to butcher livestock to lay down salted meat for the winter months and the latter for obvious meteorological reasons. It was at this time of year that fishing stopped and even today sailing enthusiasts lay up their boats for the winter months as the seas become too dangerous for small craft to venture far.

Remembrance Sunday is of course observed on the closest Sunday to 11 November (the anniversary of the signing of the armistice at the end of World War 1). This year the event will have especial poignancy as we mark the 100th anniversary of the outbreak of that war.

A happier November date in America is that of Thanksgiving, one of the most widely celebrated US holidays. It dates from the time of the Pilgrim Fathers in the 17th century and was fixed as a public holiday in 1941. Families gather together and traditionally a meal including roast turkey and pumpkin pie is eaten.

Here in Britain, November 5th is Bonfire Night, when the old rhyme tells us to ….

"Remember, remember the fifth of November, Gunpowder, treason and plot!"

On 5th November 1605 the conspirator Guy Fawkes or Guido Fawkes as he also liked to be known was arrested following one of the most audacious attempts at an act of political terrorism in British history. He and his fellow-conspirators planned to blow up the Houses of Parliament during the state opening ceremony attended by King James I (VI of Scotland). The Gunpowder Plot, as it came to be known, was only foiled because one of the plotters warned a family member not to attend Parliament that day.

A final November date to remember is the 30th, feast day of St Andrew, patron saint of Scotland. He was martyred for his faith on an X-shaped cross - as on the saltire - the Scottish flag.

BUSTLE & SEW
LOVE TO SEW AND SEW WITH LOVE

Movember Hoops

Movember is an annual event involving the growing of moustaches during the month of November to raise awareness of men's health issues, such as prostate cancer and other associated charities.

The goal of Movember is to "change the face of men's health." And here at Bustle & Sew we're helping do our bit with our two little Movember animals - a rather sophisticated cat with a monocle and a very debonair dog.

Shown mounted in 6" hoops.

Materials

For both hoops you will need:

- Four 8" x 4" pieces of quilting weight cotton
- Scraps of fabric or felt in browns, creams, green, black, pale pink, white and red
- Stranded cotton floss in black, white, dark blue, pale pink and red
- Bondaweb
- Embroidery foot for your sewing machine.
- Black and a light coloured sewing thread
- Two x 6" hoops
- Temporary fabric marker pen

Note: 2 strands of floss are used throughout except for tiny white stitch to highlight eyes.

Method

- Cut each rectangle of fabric into two 4" squares. Join 4 squares together to make one 7½" piece. Press all seams open at back to minimise bulk.

- Centre your inner hoop on top of the fabric and draw around the outside with your temporary fabric marker pen. This will give you a guide line for creating your design so it fits nicely inside your hoop. Transfer the text using your preferred method.

- Using the reversed templates trace applique pieces onto the paper side of your Bondaweb. Allow a little extra at the bottom of the body shapes so they will "disappear" into the hoop when framed. Cut out roughly, fuse onto the reverse side of your fabric and cut out carefully. Use long smooth strokes with your scissors. You will achieve the best results if you hold the scissors steady and move the fabric around. Work from the bottom forwards - start with the main body pieces and finish with the moustaches. (1)

- When you're happy with the positioning of each shape fuse into place with a hot iron. You may wish to protect your work with a piece of material. If the applique fabric is quite thick it is a good idea to press again from behind to make sure they're properly adhered to the base fabric since if they move while you're machining you won't achieve a nice finish.

- When you're happy with the positioning of your pieces fit the embroidery foot to your machine and with black thread in the needle and a light colour in the bobbin stitch around pieces as shown. (2) Remember you are aiming for a sort of scribbled effect, go around each piece twice and don't be too neat!

- To finish dog draw mouth and centre line of nose in with your temporary marker pen and machine stitch. Eyes are a few small straight stitches in tblack floss highlighted with a tiny white stitch. Stitch text in back stitch worked in blue floss.

- To finish cat draw in eyebrow and machine stitch. Then draw in and add monocle in chain stitch glass in running stitch and the monocle cord is a single long stitch in blue. Eyes as dog. Stitch text in back stitch and red floss.

- Remove temporary lines and press lightly on reverse. Mount in hoops. FINISHED!

Pop over to Etsy and get your hands on a gorgeous cable knitted lampshade from Buubok. All handmade, these shades are sure to add some extra cosy to your home this Winter!

Luuba Lightshade, Buubok www.etsy.com

Catherine Tough Ladies Lambswool
Socks, Cotswold Trading
www.cotswoldtrading.com

Beginner's Pompom Hat Knitting Kit,
Not on the High Street
www.notonthehighstreet.com

Chunky Wool Beige Oatmeal Scarf,
The Nautical Company
www.thenauticalcompany.com

Harris Tweed Clock Macleod
Tartan, Juniper & Jane
www.juniperandjane.co.uk

Feeling Cosy!

Keep away those chills with these gorgeous snuggly accessories

Owl Knitted Booties,
Prezzybox.com
www.prezzybox.com

Warm Brown Throw, Tesco
www.Tesco.com

Winter Woodland Cushion,
Sophie Allport
www.sophieallport.com

Katie Alice Highland Fling
Teapot, Creative Tops
www.creative-tops.com

Top Five Tips for Etsy sellers

make your shop the best it possibly can be this year!

November sees the start of the busiest time of year for small business owners and online crafters across the globe. Many choose to sell their creations through sites such as Etsy and Folksy – but what should you do to make sure your shop stands out from the crowd this year?

Whether you're just starting out, or have been around for a while, you're sure to find some useful advice in our top five tips for Etsy (or Folksy) selling success!

1 Make your shop a great place to visit. Create an attractive look and feel and make sure your brand identity shines through. If you're new to selling online, then start off with a selection of your best and most popular designs to give your new customers the best possible impression of your brand. You can always increase the number of products you have listed as your shop becomes more established.

2 Take a good hard look at your competition. See who else is selling similar products, and check to see how much they're charging - and if they're making sales at those prices. Aim for prices that reflect your time and skills. Remember to include the hidden extras - as well as time taken making each article, and costs of materials, include time taken to photograph and present each listing as well as fees, packaging and other less obvious costs.

3 Make sure your photography is up to scratch. Attractive, professional-looking images will give your shop an advantage over other sellers. Take your photographs in natural light or against white backgrounds - bright, clear images are most attractive online. Don't be afraid to experiment with props to find the best way to present your products.

4 Regularly update your shop. This will encourage your customers to revisit, as new items are automatically added to their feeds. Try to do a little maintenance often - two or three times each week. Re-list any sold items if you have more in stock, keep your descriptions updated and change the photographs for a fresh, exciting feel.

5 Don't forget to market. Remember, your Etsy shop isn't like being on the High Street, there simply isn't any "passing trade." Facebook and Twitter are great ways to spread the word about your shop, as well as curating treasuries and joining Etsy groups.

Happy selling this Christmas time!

Christmas Reindeer Softie

I'm not sure if this little reindeer is Rudolph, Robert or their cousin Richard, but whatever you decide to name him, he's the cutest little reindeer you'll discover this Christmas - we think so anyway!

Our little reindeer is handsewn from felt with shiny bead eyes and a little red button nose. The only slightly fiddly part is sewing in his antlers and ears, but it's quite easy if you take your time. He's finished off with a nice warm scarf simply cut from a piece of old plaid blanket.

Reindeer measures 9" tall approx

Materials

- 12" square brown felt
- 6" square cream felt
- 6" square black felt
- 3" x 2" pale pink felt
- 12" x ¾" strip of fabric for scarf
- 2 small spherical black beads
- Small button for nose
- Stranded cotton floss in brown (to match felt), cream, pale pink and black
- Cream sewing thread
- Toy stuffing

You will find a stuffing stick really useful when making softies. Mine is just a bamboo skewer with the pointed end broken off and frayed a little. This means it will "grab" the stuffing and give you more control, especially when stuffing small parts. Be sure to add your stuffing in small pieces and shape the softie with your hands as you work. This will avoid lumpiness.

This reindeer needs stuffing quite firmly to keep his shape and make sure his legs aren't bendy, but don't overfill and distort the shape.

Method

- Cut out all pieces from the templates (full size)

- Place ear inners on top of outer ears and stitch in place using small straight stitches in 2 strands of pink floss. Insert your needle at an angle so the floss doesn't show on the wrong side of the ear, and your stitch is hidden in the thickness of the felt.

- With right sides facing outwards join the under-gussets to the main body around the legs from D to E using two strands of brown floss and working in half cross-stitch first in one direction, then back along the seam in the other direction to complete the stitches. This gives a strong decorative finish.

- Join the two muzzle pieces together along the top and bottom edges from X to B around nose tip by placing the two pieces right sides together and using a small back stitch. Alternatively you can machine stitch if preferred. Turn right side out so the seam is inside the muzzle. (1)

- Join the antlers with cross stitch using cream floss and stuffing firmly as you go. At the bottom pinch the two seams together and secure with a few stitches. This is important so that when you insert them in the head seam they will remain upright. (2)

- Join the two parts of the body together from E to B with cross stitch.

- Insert head gusset between A and C, adding ears (folded in half) and antlers as you go. (1 and 2)

- Stuff head lightly so it's easier to work with. Stuff end of muzzle then push onto head matching X and B then secure to head with small straight stitches in cream floss. Pull stuffing out of head, then stuff properly.

- Join body halves from D to T, folding tail in half and inserting at T.

- Stuff legs firmly. Close back seam, stuffing body as you go pushing firmly into place with your stuffing stick as the gap gets smaller.

- Stitch the hoof pieces into pairs using cross stitch and black floss. Push onto bottoms of legs and secure in place with small straight stitches in black floss.

- Sew nose button into place and add eyes. Take your time with the eyes, testing their position with glass-headed pins as this will make an enormous difference to your softie's expression. Secure the eyes in place with long stitches right through the head, pulling slightly on the thread to shape the eye sockets.

- Fringe ends of your scarf fabric and tie around neck.

- Your reindeer is now finished!

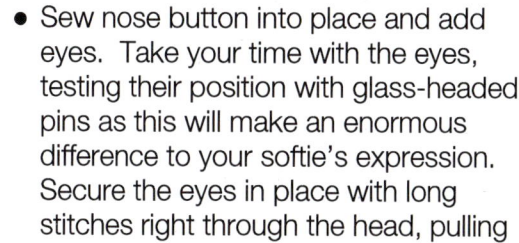

Simple Crochet Flowers

Materials:
> DMC Petra 3 in 54518 (powder blue), 5151 (pearl pink), 53849 (mermaid blue) and 53608 (magenta), mint (5772), golden (5742).
> 2.5mm Crochet Hook
> Darning Needle

Crochet Terms Used (UK)
> Ch - Chain
> Sl St - Slip Stitch
> Dc - Double Crochet
> Tr - Treble Crochet
> FLO - Front Loops Only. To work in the front loops only, look at the V created from the previous stitches. Then dc into the side closest to yourself, dc as normal. Basically you are dc onto one loop, rather than the two as normal.

Pattern:

Round one -

Ch6, sl st to join to form a ring.

Round two -

Ch3 (1st tr), then 23tr into ring. (24). Sl st to join.

Round three -

Ch1, 1dc in same st. 1dc into each FLO of all sts. Sl st to first dc to join.

Round four -

Ch1, 1dc in same st. Work *(1htr, 1tr, 1dtr) into next st, repeat in next st, 1dc into next st. Repeat from * 7 more times. Omit last 1dc in last sts. Sl st to join. Cut yarn and sew in ends.

messyla

Lara is a blogger, freelance stylist and photographer living in Scotland who spends her days snapping away, conjuring up delicious recipes, crocheting flowers, foods & animals or writing.

Be sure to check out Lara's gorgeous website www.messyla.com and follow her on Instagram @messyla.

Machine Applique - freestyle and very easy!

This month I've included three patterns that use freestyle machine embroidery and raw edge applique. I love this method as it gives great results in a remarkably short period of time – perfect if you're working to a deadline, or if (like Rosie and me) you're trying to give lots of handmade gifts this Christmas. I know many people are a little nervous of trying this technique, I most definitely was, but now I love working in this way – I view my sewing machine in a whole new light as not just a method of joining pieces of fabric together, but as a means of creative expression in its own right.

You don't need any expensive equipment for this technique – you'll almost certainly have everything you need already. You will need a sewing machine of course – but it doesn't need to be expensive and/or fancy. In fact the simpler the better as you will only need to use the basic straight stitch option.

Use sharp scissors to cut out your applique shapes. I use my large shears which seems perhaps a little odd when I'm often cutting fairly small shapes, but for me it's easier to make long smooth curving cuts with their long blades as I don't have to stop and open them again all the time. I also have a small pair of sharp scissors that are good for cutting very tiny curves, like the twirls on the cat's movember moustache.

Many people like to hoop up before starting their machine applique. I personally don't do this as I prefer to work without. (unlike hand embroidery where I simply can't stitch without one!). If you do decide to use a hoop then, like hand embroidery, be sure to choose a good brand that will secure your fabric tightly. An 8" or 20 cm hoop is a good versatile size.

If you become really enthusiastic about this technique you'll find yourself jealously hoarding even the smallest fabric scraps in case they come in useful for one of your creations. Almost all sorts of fabrics work well including scraps from previous projects, old clothes or treasures from thrift or charity shops. Do avoid stretchy fabric though, as well as fabrics with a very loose weave as they will fray and distort. Quilting weight cotton is the perfect choice, whilst choose a heavier fabric (such as Kidston cotton duck) for the background as it will need to support a lot of stitching.

Normal thread is perfect for the actual machine stitching. You can choose a dark thread for the needle so your stitches will stand out, or perhaps a contrasting colour if you want to add some complementary stitching. Use a pale colour in the bobbin to give you a less solid stitching line as you're aiming for a sort of scribbled effect, not strong black lines on your fabric.

Buttons, braids and embroidery floss are the final elements of your kit box. It's nice to embellish your work and I think that adding touches of hand embroidery makes it both more personal and also rather special – unlike anything you'll find in the shops.

YOUR MACHINE

When using this technique you'll need to fit the darning foot to your sewing machine. This will help stop your fabric puckering as you stitch whilst protecting your fingers as you move your work around freely. You'll also need to drop the feed dogs. When these are up in their normal position they grip and feed the fabric in a straight line beneath your needle as you stitch. When they're dropped you can mover your fabric around freely in any direction. The method of dropping your feed dogs will vary between machines, so if you're uncertain then just check your manufacturer's guide.

I haven't found it necessary to alter the tension on my machine for freestyle stitching, just make these two small easy adjustments.

START STITCHING

If you're new to this method, then it's a good idea to practise before starting your project. Being able to confidently outline your applique shapes is crucial to your success. It's not hard, but is a very different feel to normal machine sewing. You have to imagine that you're drawing the shape with your sewing machine needle, but instead of moving a pencil over paper, you're moving the paper – or, in this case, the fabric. It feels really odd to be able to move your fabric in all directions beneath the needle and it does take some practice, so don't expect to become an expert straight away. Like most skills, the more you practise, the better you'll become!

Fit your darning/embroidery foot and thread your machine in the usual way. Drop your feed dogs. Hoop your fabric if preferred. Place fabric under the needle and drop the foot. Lower the needle into the fabric before beginning to stitch – this isn't an essential step but I find it gives me more control. Set your machine to straight stitch. The actual length of the stitch will be controlled by the movement of the hoop.

Begin to sew slowly, controlling the machine's speed with your foot. Move the fabric around to create some scribbly lines – don't worry too much about the effect, this is only practising – but think about how it feels to use your machine in this very different way. As your confidence grows you can increase the sewing speed to a nice steady middling sort of pace so your stitched lines will flow smoothly.

When you feel comfortable with your needle speed and with moving the fabric in different directions try outlining some simple shapes with the needle. You can try freehand or draw shapes onto your practice fabric to stitch over. Remember – you can move your fabric in any direction. Outlining a shape twice is very attractive and there's no need to be too neat, you are aiming for a nice scribbled effect. As your confidence grows try more complicated shapes and don't be scared of "getting it wrong" – you're only practising at the moment. Just keep everything simple and remember that wobbly lines are very attractive when combined with nice fabrics in this technique.

APPLIQUE TECHNIQUE

If you think of your stitching lines as drawing with pencil, then you're "colouring in" your drawings with your choices of fabrics. This isn't beautifully neat turned edge applique, but is a much more spontaneous technique that relies on finding exactly the right fabric for your design. The applique itself is very simple – just trace the template shapes onto the paper side of your Bondaweb, cut out roughly, then fuse to the reverse of your fabric. Carefully cut out the shapes along the lines you trace using long smooth cuts with large scissors or shears. Hold the scissors steady in one hand then turn the fabric as you cut. Cutting this way will give you much more control than trying to move the scissors around the fabric. When you've cut out your shape, peel off the paper backing, position on the background fabric and fuse in place with a hot iron, protecting your work with a cloth if necessary. Lots of Bustle & Sew designs use layered applique shapes. In this case you will need to work from the bottom or back upwards and cut a little extra on the underneath shapes so they will be overlapped by the shapes above – no ugly gaps in between.

FABRIC CHOICES

Choose a nice plain or discreetly patterned medium weight fabric for your background. It must be non-stretchy and natural fibres are nicest to work with. Take a look at furnishing fabrics, cotton twills and ducks are perfect. When choosing fabrics for both the background and the applique work ask yourself will the completed work need to be washed? If so, you'll need to make sure all your choices are colour-fast and won't shrink – consider pre-washing to be certain.

For applique fabrics stick to natural fibres that won't stretch when stitched or melt when you fuse your shapes to the background. Quilting weight cotton is absolutely perfect to start with as it's really easy to use. As you gain experience it's fun to experiment with different types of fabric.

Consider also whether the fabric will fray – a little bit of fraying can be very attractive, but if the weave is too loose or unstable you won't be able to work with it properly. Also think about pattern sizes. It's best to choose fabrics with small scale patterns that can be seen when you've cut out your shapes – you'll lose the effect of larger prints. Have a rummage around the bargain bins at your fabric shop for nice remnants, many designs use only very small amounts of each print.

AND FINALLY

Most of all relax and have fun! Choose good quality materials, working with cheap and nasty fabrics will give poor results – and a lot of frustration along the way! If things aren't going very well, then take a break and return refreshed.

HAPPY STITCHING!

Friends Forever Hoop Art

This design is a great make if you're just starting out in hand embroidery or freestyle machine applique as the bird shapes are really easy both to cut and to applique into place whilst the text is simply stitched in back stitch.

A nice extra special touch is the baker's twine for the birds to perch on, held in place by their feet.

Make the whole flock, or this design would be fun to adapt for familes or couples - just change the number and sizes of birds.

Shown mounted in a 10" hoop.

Materials

- 12" square medium weight background fabric
- Stranded cotton floss in blue, green, black, white, golden brown and red
- 12" length baker's twine
- Scraps of felt and cotton fabric
- Temporary fabric marker pen
- Bondaweb

- Embroidery foot for your sewing machine
- Black thread for the needle and a pale colour for the bobbin
- 10" embroidery hoop

Method

- Transfer the design to the centre of your fabric using your preferred method. You can omit transferring the birds, but doing so does help with the correct placing of your pieces.

- Using the reversed template trace the applique shapes onto the paper side of your Bondaweb. Allow extra on the bottom shape where they overlap. Fuse onto the reverse of your fabric and cut out carefully.

- Working from the bottom or back upwards position your shapes on the background fabric. When you're happy with their positioning fuse into place with a hot iron, protecting your work with a cloth if necessary.

- With your temporary fabric marker pen draw in the position of the eyes, feet and baker's twine. (1)

- Fit the embroidery foot to your sewing machine and drop the feed dogs. With black or another dark colour in the needle and a pale colour in the bobbin go around the outline of each shape twice in a sort of scribbled effect.

- Stitch the birds' eyes in 2 strands of black floss - just a few small straight stitches, then add a tiny highlight with a single strand of white floss. Stitch beaks in 2 strands of golden brown floss.

- Work text in 3 strands of floss and back stitch. I chose blue for the words TRUE and STAY, red for FRIENDS FOREVER and green for TOGETHER as these colours worked well with my fabric choices. Have a look at your birds and choose the colours that work with your fabrics.

- Lay the baker's twine along the line you drew with your temporary fabric marker pen and overstitch (or couch) the birds' feet - these are just a few straight stitches worked over the twine to keep it in place.

- Remove all temporary lines and press your work lightly on the reverse.

- Mount your work in the hoop. There isn't really any need to secure the ends of the twine as they will be held in place by the hoop, but if you're at all concerned then secure with a few stitches.

- FINISHED!

Apple & Blackberry Loaf Cake

Ingredients

> 1½ cups plain flour
> 1 cup brown sugar
> 175g butter
> ½ tsp cinnamon
> 1 tbsp baking powder
> 1 small red apple, cored and grated (leave skin on)
> 2 eggs, lightly beaten
> 1½ cups blackberries, divided

This scrumptious loaf cake is relatively simple and straightforward to make, but the taste is incredible and will impress all guests, young and old!

Prep Time	Cook Time	Total Time
20 mins	1 hr 20 mins	2 hrs 40 mins

Instructions

> Preheat oven to 180°C/350°F/Gas Mark 4. Line a 12cm x 25cm loaf pan with baking paper. In a large bowl, add plain flour, brown sugar and butter and use fingers to rub into pea-sized pieces. Scoop 5 tablespoons of mixture into a separate small bowl and mix in cinnamon. Set aside. This will be the streusel topping. Returning to the large bowl, add baking powder and combine well.

> In a separate medium bowl, combine grated apple and lightly beaten eggs. Add to large bowl of flour

mixture and stir until just combined, then gently fold in 1 cup of blackberries.

> Pour mixture into prepared loaf pan and evenly sprinkle remaining blackberries on top, followed by streusel topping. Bake for 1 hour 20 minutes, until a skewer inserted into the middle comes out clean. If cake is browning too much, cover with aluminium foil for the last 20-30 minutes. Allow cake to cool in pan for 20 minutes, then move to a wire rack to cool completely.

> To keep the outside crisp and inside moist, store cake wrapped in baking paper, then aluminium foil inside an airtight container.

CLOSE ENCOUNTERS OF THE COOKING KIND

We chat to Alice from Close Encounters of The Coking Kind - an Aussie living in London who moved to England almost 3 years ago chasing love and an adventure...

When did you first start making and baking cakes?

I had made a few cakes here and there since I was a teenager, and I'm sure there were a few that I helped mum with as a kid, but it's only really been in the last year or two that I've really gotten into baking.

Can you remember the first cake you ever made?

I can't remember the first cake I ever made, but it probably involved helping my mum by licking the beaters! I remember the first cupcake recipe I made on my own was a basic vanilla cupcake with strawberry icing. They weren't anything fancy, but they were delicious!

When and why did you decide to start your blog?

I started my blog last October in an effort to improve my cooking and baking and to expand my recipe base, as I was getting bored of the same old recipes. If I want to keep posting recipes on my blog, I have to keep trying new recipes, so it's been a great way of getting me out of my comfort zone and trying new things.

Do you have a favourite baker who inspires you?

I don't really have any favourites, but I'm impressed with Mary Berry and how she is still working hard to encourage everyone to get in the kitchen and bake at almost 80. She has become the face of baking in the UK and inspired generations of people to bake.

What's your favourite recipe on your blog?

This is a tough one! I'll have to give a savoury and a sweet one, because I can't choose between them. My favourite sweet recipe on Close Encounters of the Cooking Kind would have to be my Chocolate Mud Cake because it reminds me of every birthday growing up and my favourite savoury recipe is my Marinated Chinese Chicken and Vegetable Stir Fry because I love Chinese food so much!

Be sure to pop over to Ailice's blog, www.closeencountersofthecookingkind.com for lots more delicious recipes and gorgeous baking inspiration!

Belle & Boo Winter Tin, One Brown Cow
www.onebrowncow.co.uk

Folk Art Hand Painted Measuring Cups, The Oak Room
www.oakroomshop.co.uk

Red Heart Tea Towel, Berry Red
www.berryred.co.uk

Mixing Bowl, Mason Cash
www.masoncash.co.uk

Star Baker

Whip up a storm in the kitchen with these lovely baking goodies!

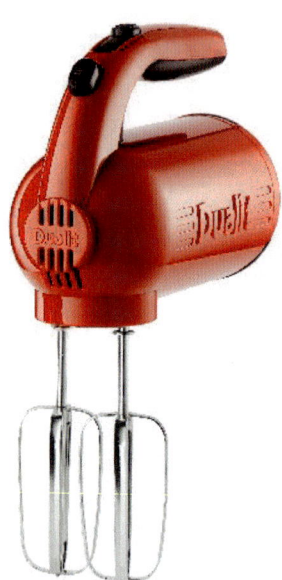

Dualit Red Hand Mixer, Red Candy
www.redcandy.co.uk

Stag Oven Glove, Sophie Allport
www.sophieallport.com

Cream Scales, Contento Shop
www.contento-shop.com

Baked With Love Cake Stand, The Contemporary Home
www.tch.net

Embroidered Floral Alphabet

As well as full instructions for stitching the letters A and Z and making the bookends shown, I've included templates for the whole alphabet, plus an ampersand.

They are hand drawn and I haven't included detailed instructions for stitching them, as to do so would need a whole book I think! But that's part of the fun of freehand embroidery.

Each letter measures 4 ½" tall and the bookends measure 6" h x 4 ½" w x 2" d.

Materials for Bookends

- Two x 7" squares cream linen or linen blend fabric
- 1 FQ or a little less of gingham
- 3 A4 or Letter size pieces of light weight card
- Polybeads/rice or similar to weight your bookends
- Toy stuffing
- DMC stranded cotton floss in colours 156, 309, 341, 502, 520, 605, 906, 3835, 4077
- Sticky tape (sellotape)

On the next pages you'll find stitching instructions for the A and Z only. It should be fairly easy to apply these directions to the other letters as they're all drawn in the same way.

Notes on Stitching

Two strands of floss are used throughout and the templates are given actual size.

The leaves and buds are very simply stitched in back and straight stitch.

The blue french knots have 2 twists.

The large pink and blue flowers are stitched as follows: start with 3855 and work radiating straight stitches around a central point, then surround these with further straight stitches in either 341 or 605. Finish with a tiny single twist French knot in 4077.

The long buds are two or three parallel bullion stitches and the roses are also bullion stitch.

Bullion stitch

Fly stitch

When you have finished stitching your letters press your work lightly on the reverse being careful not to flatten the stitches. Then trim the cream fabric to a 5" x 6 ½" rectangle.

Seam allowance for bookends is ¼"

Stop stitching 1/4" before end of fabric

Making your Bookends

Please note, directions are for one bookend only, you make them both in the same way.

- From your gingham fabric cut one 5" x 6½" rectangle, two 5" x 2 ½" rectangles and two 6 ½ " x 2 ½" rectangles.

- From your card cut two 4 ½" x 6" rectangles, two 4 ½" x 2" rectangles and two 6" x 2 " rectangles.

- Join the card into a three-sided box with sellotape leaving the bottom side open (1). This will be the liner for your bookend, stopping it from being too rounded when you stuff it.

- With right sides together join the 2 ½" wide rectangles to the sides of your embroidery by machine. Stop stitching ¼" before the end of each seam - this is the secret of a nice neat rectangle ensuring all your pieces will meet at a crisp corner. (2 and 3)

- Add the large rectangle for the back in the same way leaving the bottom edge open for stuffing (4).

- Stuff with toy stuffing at the top, adding polybeads/rice at the bottom, finishing off with some more stuffing.

- Slip stitch the bottom seam closed. Repeat for second book end.

- Add books and enjoy!

- FINISHED!!

Meet the Maker

"There is no better feeling than people buying your work and getting joy from what you've designed"

Catherine Beaumont talks to us about sewing, fabric design and how she started her lifestyle brand, Peonie Cole

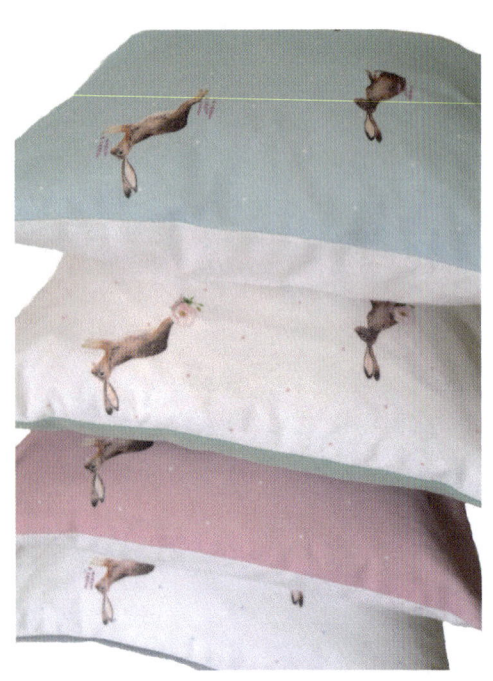

Inspired by the beautiful Scottish Borders Countryside and Northumbrian Coastline, Catherine creates beautiful fabrics, homeware and cards featuring her hand painted designs that celebrate the colour and beauty of British nature.

How did you get into crafting?

My Mum and my Granny were always very into crafts such as sewing, embroidery and tapestry. I always promised myself that by the time I had my own children I would need to be able to make dressing-up costumes as good as the ones my Mum made for me! Studying textile design furthered my interest in sewing as I was always keen to make new things out of the fabrics I was designing. I am still learning and enjoy creating new products to add to my existing range.

How did your business come about?

I realised quite quickly after I graduated that I really wanted to sell my work under my own name and not work for a big design company. I visited the Country Living Fair in London and fell in love with the idea of having a stand there and selling my work. I really hope this dream can become a reality in the next few years! Since moving to the Scottish Borders last year I have been inspired by my surroundings to produce new collections, include my new Countryside Animals range, and really create my brand around my country lifestyle.

Which are your favourite designs?

I love my Peony and Bee design as I think it sums up my huge love for my favourite flowers- hydrangeas and peonies. I used details from the design in my wedding stationery, which I designed myself, so I think it will always hold a special place in my heart.

Have you had any crafting disasters?

Luckily I have managed to avoid any huge crafting disasters although I can get slightly excited when working on a new product

idea and this excitement mixed with a bit of impatience means that my first attempt can sometimes turn out a little odd! I am learning to take my time though - I will get there one day!

Why do you think there has been a resurgence in homemade/handmade?

I think there has been a big resurgence in crafting and homemade goods as I feel there has been a step away from mass-produced items with people realising that they can create one-off, quality, special things themselves. It is now easier than ever to find crafting inspiration out there with books, magazines (like Bustle & Sew!) and online with Pinterest and Youtube that people can get information from a huge number of sources and starting making things at home easily.

For our wedding we asked some of our friends to give us gifts which they had hand-made themselves instead of gift-list items. We have ended up with some truly beautiful works of art using so many techniques ranging from embroidery, cross-stitch, painting, collage and laser-cut wood! All these items are completely one-off and priceless to us and really emphasise the wonderful, special nature of hand-crafted goods.

What advice would you give to anyone who wants to turn their hobby into a business?

There is never a better time to do it and you don't want to look back in 10 years and wonder what if! For me there is no better feeling than people buying your work and getting joy from what you have designed.

What do you think the trends will be for Christmas 2014 and beyond?

I think animal prints, berries and foliage will be popular this Christmas with lots of rich shades of red and metallic accents like golds and silvers. Florals of course are always in fashion and I see that continuing into 2015. I love that there is always a floral out there for everyone!

Peonie Cole

Peonie Cole is a fresh and floral lifestyle brand with an increasing range of fabrics, homeware and cards featuring designs that celebrate the colour and beauty of British nature.

www.peoniecole.co.uk
@peoniecoletextiles

Look! a lovely idea
Deer Art Print

Hot foot it over to Graffical Muse and download this gorgeous print. Best of all, lovely Leslie is giving it away totally FREE!!

Image and FREE Download: www.grafficalmuse.com

Candy Cone Mouse

This little mouse and his cone measure 8" long from the bottom of the Cone (excluding bell) to the tip of the mouse's ears.

Fill his cone with candy and little mouse will resist every temptation to nibble before Christmas morning!

He also makes a great little pocket toy when all the candy has gone and Christmas is over.

Materials

- 6" square grey felt
- 10" x 8" Christmasssy fabric for cone exterior
- 10" x 8" felt for cone lining
- 9" ric rac braid
- Three ¼" buttons for shoulders and tail
- One very small button for nose (if you can't find one, then you can stitch nose with black floss)
- Decorative red button (mine was heart shaped)
- Black embroidery floss for eyes
- Black or dark brown strong thread for whiskers
- Small bell for base of cone (optional)
- Small quantity of toy stuffing
- 8" length of ¼" wide ribbon for hanging cone
- Grey thread

Method

- Cut out all pieces from the full size template. Additionally cut a strip of felt 5" x ¼" for the mouse's tail. Give this strip one pointy end.

Cone

- Turn over ¼" at top edge of exterior cone and press down. (1) Trim 3/8" from top edge of felt interior. Place exterior wrong side up on clean flat surface then position interior on top aligning top edge so it is 1/8" lower than the folded edge of the exterior fabric. Pin or tack, then stitch ric rac braid around top of the interior so it just peeps out (2)

- Fold cone right sides inwards with long edge together and machine stitch seam with a ¼" allowance. Clip point and turn right side out. Trim away exterior fabric at top of seam and with matching thread oversew the interior felt to hide the raw edge (3)

- Add hanging loop with a few stitches and cover join with decorative button (4)

- Stitch bell to bottom of cone and part-fill with toy stuffing

Mouse

- Machine sew main body piece together with a 1/8" seam allowance. Clip curves and turn right side out. Stuff the head, neck and top part of the boy firmly and the bottom of the body quite lightly, stopping your stuffing ½" from the bottom.

- With front and back seams matching stitch along bottom edge of body (5)

- Pinch corners together and stitch to make little feet (6)

- Attach arms adding small button at shoulders.

- Form a curve by overlapping the sides of the notch at the bottom of the ear shapes and stitch into place on the head.

- Attach tail to base of body and secure with button.

- Sew black eyes and insert whiskers. To do this take a nice long length of strong thread and double it in your needle. Push the needle into one side of the nose and bring it out at the tip, leaving a 1" tail of thread sticking out. Make a tiny back stitch at the nose and bring your needle out on the other side of the nose. Take it in again leaving a loop and repeat. When you have enough whiskers, fasten off and trim loops. Add button to cover back stitches at nose tip.

- Place mouse in cone and add candy. FINISHED!!

Help keep your workroom tidy with this gorgeous crochet basket. Perfect for stashing yarn or leftover fabric scraps - being tidy never looked so cute!

Look!
a lovely idea

Foxy Basket

Image from All About Ami: http://www.allaboutami.com/post/82237092962/foxbasket

Waste not Want not

A little forethought and planning can save you money around the home - and is kind for the environment as well as your purse!

If you grow your own herbs, trim them during the summer when they begin to overtake the garden and dry the trimmings by hanging them upside down in bunches in the kitchen. They add a natural touch, smell lovely and you can use them for stocks and sauces.

We're all familiar with "Make do and Mend"

Take a look around your garden too

When you have a glut of apples store them carefully for winter use. I put mine between layers of newspaper, being careful they don't touch each other - this spreads down the spread of any mould. They do need to be kept in a cool place like your shed or garage as they deteriorate quickly in a centrally heated house.

If you have honesty growing in your garden, don't weed it out but pick it in the autumn. Slide off the husks around the beautiful white round heads and use them in dried flower arrangements.

Indoors try using leftover wall paper to line kitchen shelves and chests of drawers. For the larder shelf cut half a dozen layers to size and remove a layer regularly as it becomes soiled

Keep leftover wallpaper to patch any damaged areas. Cut out a matching piece slightly larger than the area you need to replace - leaving the edge slightly irregular will make the patch less noticeable. Glue to the spot, matching the pattern carefully and using a roller to flatten the edges.

You can increase the life span of a sponge mop considerably by storing the sponge end with a plastic bag tied around it to stop it drying out and warping. Save on detergent by adding a tablespoon of bicarbonate of soda to the wash - this also softens the water, And soften dried-out shoe polish with a little turpentine to give it a new lease of life.

Save energy with foil! Line your grill pan with foil to reflect heat. This has a dual purpose - not only does it save energy, but is useful in that you can discard it after use rather than having to scrub grease and other deposits off the pan. You can also place a sheet of foil under your ironing board cover to reflect the heat of the iron back into the garments and make an often much-disliked task faster and easier!

Keep plastic containers (eg margarine, ice cream and yoghurt) and use for storing and freezing food. You can also use them for all sorts of other purposes - I like to recycle them into containers for cleaning paintbrushes and/or mixing paint as again they don't have to be cleaned, but can simply be discarded after use.

And finally .. Old toothbrushes are amazingly useful for all sorts of tasks around the home, including cleaning jewellery, scrubbing limescale and deposits off taps, dipped in bleach to clean tile grouting, and polishing intricate mouldings as well as getting into the nooks and crannies of all kinds of equipment.

Rich Days

Welcome to you, rich Autumn days,
Ere comes the cold, leaf-picking wind;
When golden stocks are seen in fields,
All standing arm-in-arm entwined;
And gallons of sweet cider seen
On trees in apples red and green.

With mellow pears that cheat our teeth,
Which melt that tongues may suck them in,
With blue-black damsons, yellow plums,
And wood nuts rich, to make us go
Into the loneliest lanes we know.

W H Davies

November's Favourite Blogs

Little Cotton Rabbits
Julie blogs about knitting and life with an autistic son.

So September
Lovely embroidery and design - eye candy and stitching too!

Butter Baking
Only a one-word description needed - yummy!

Dottie Angel
Quirky vintage-led blog.

42

Applique Village Shade

The final pattern in this month's magazine is a first for Bustle & Sew - an applique lampshade. I've recently discovered really easy lampshade making kits from Needcraft, and with the nights drawing in it seemed like the perfect time to try them out.

The applique is really easy - if a little fiddly in places as the pieces are quite small, and the shade is beyond easy to assemble - the kit comes with full instructions and even a link to a how-to-video. My shade measured 30 cm (12" approx diameter and 21 cm (just over 8" tall).

Materials

- 1 yard x 8" neutral coloured medium weight fabric
- 1 yard x 4" green dotty medium weight fabric
- Lots of cotton scraps
- Bondaweb
- Embroidery foot
- Black thread for needle & light colour for bobbin.
- Lampshade making kit - mine was manufactured by Needcraft and I purchased it from Amazon. You can also purchase from the Needcraft website

Method

- Join your two strips of background fabric along one long edge using a ¼" seam allowance. Press seam open at back to minimise bulk (1)

- Fold in half and press fold with your hands (don't use an iron as you don't want a permanent crease in your finished shade).

- Using the fold as a guide to the centre line, cut out your applique houses and position them on shade. The bottoms of the houses should be just a little beneath the seam between the two fabrics. (2)

- When you're happy with the positioning press with a hot iron to adhere the pieces.

- Fit the embroidery foot to your sewing machine and drop the feed dogs. With black thread in your needle and a pale thread in your bobbin outline the shapes going around twice for a scribbled effect. Add frames to the windows in the same way (3)

- Continue until the design is complete. The railings are two lines of machine stitching - if you're not confident to work these by eye, then draw in stitching lines with a temporary fabric marker pen (4).

- When your design is complete press lightly on the reverse. (5)

- Remove any tails of thread and make up shade according to instructions on kit.

Transferring your pattern

Possibly the most frequent query I receive is "How do I transfer my embroidery design from the printed page to my fabric?" This is one of those questions where there isn't a single right or wrong answer – it's all about choosing the method that works best for you.

The easiest method to transfer a design is of course an iron-on transfer, many of which used to be given away free with needlework magazines in the mid-20th century, printed in either blue or silver.

My grandmother had a huge collection of these transfers, all carefully stored in a biscuit box with a cute puppy and kitten picture on the lid. There were sunbonnet and crinoline ladies - too many to count - birds, bears and an infinite variety of flower patterns. If you enjoy stitching vintage, it's still easy to find these old designs in thrift shops, at jumble sales and of course on auction sites such as eBay.

But if you don't have a transfer and want to transfer a downloaded pattern (like those in this magazine) there are several different methods available to you, some of which are easier, and so perhaps more popular, than others.

If you're embroidering onto a pale coloured, light-weight fabric, then it's easy to trace your design onto it as though it was tracing paper. To do this, print your design in the usual way, then tape your printed sheet to a light source - most usually a light box or window pane. Position your fabric over it, right side up, making sure that the design is beneath the position you have chosen for your finished embroidery.

Tape your fabric in place over the paper. Don't be tempted to try to hold it with one hand while tracing with the other - unless it's really small and simple your fabric is quite likely to slip out of position leading to frustration and a spoiled design (I am speaking from experience!). If you have some then masking tape is the best to use as it's easier to remove than sellotape and leaves less sticky residue. Use the smallest amount you actually need and keep it to the edges of your fabric, just in case.

When everything is securely held in place, trace over your design with a sharp pencil or a water soluble temporary fabric marker pen. I have read debate online about whether or not the marks from these pens can reappear over a period of time, spoiling your finished work. I haven't personally experienced this problem, but if in doubt then use a pencil. This will leave a permanent mark, but it won't bleed into other areas and should be covered by your stitching.

Another popular choice is to use dressmakers' carbon paper. This isn't at all the same as the old-fashioned carbon paper those of us of a certain age remember using when typing copies of a letter on a typewriter. *(Aside: Did you know that typewriters are no longer manufactured anywhere in the world?)* Dressmakers' carbon paper is a thicker, waxier paper and doesn't smudge. It is available in different colours to suit different fabrics. This technique is only good for smooth fabrics.

Iron the fabric you want to stitch on and then place it right side up on a clean flat surface. Tape it securely to the surface. Choose the best colour carbon paper to show up on this fabric and tape this into place shiny side down. Then position your pattern on top of the carbon paper and again, tape (or pin) it to stop it slipping around as you work. Then take a pencil or ballpoint pen and draw carefully over the lines of the pattern.

Don't press too hard or you might tear the paper and spoil the design, but press firmly enough for your lines to show up on the fabric. You might want to test this first on a corner of the fabric. Once you've traced over all the lines, remove the tape and lift off the pattern and carbon paper - your design will then be ready to stitch.

You can also purchase transfer pencils - the lines these draw will iron onto your fabric in the same way as the old-fashioned transfers. For this method you will need to print the reversed pattern. Then on your printed sheet, draw over the pattern lines with the transfer pen. The sheet can then be turned over and the design ironed onto your fabric - when of course it will be the right way round.

Prick and pounce is a time-honoured method that sounds like some kind of old-fashioned music hall act - in fact it's a very old tried and trusted method of transferring a design to fabric. It does take a little while, but is very effective. The pounce is a powder which comes in either black (crushed charcoal) or white (powdered cuttlefish - yes really!) - or you can mix the two to make grey.

You can purchase a special pad to apply the pounce, or make your own from a rolled up piece of felt. Then trace your design onto tracing paper and lay it on a folded cloth or ironing board. With a hat pin, pin in cork, or even another special tool you can purchase just for this purpose, prick a series of small holes closely together all along the design lines. Then tape your fabric onto a flat board or working surface and tape the pricked tracing paper onto the fabric. Dip your pad into the pounce powder and, with a circular motion, gently rub the pounce over the design.

Complete the whole design before removing the pricked tracing paper in a single nice clean movement. If you brush the pounce from the pricked paper it can be reused indefinitely. Now, following the pounce outline, paint a fine line all along the dotted outlines on the fabric, using a brush and watercolour paint, or very fine marker. Then un-tape and shake your fabric to remove the pounce.

Tacking through tissue paper is another a time-honoured, fairly time consuming, method of transferring your design. It is great in that it leaves absolutely no marks on your fabric and is suitable for all kinds of fabric.

Carefully trace your design onto tissue paper. Then position your tracing on top of the fabric and secure in place around the edges. Tack around the outline starting and finishing your line securely. Make sure the stitches are not too small or they will be hard to remove, and not too big so that you miss parts of the design.

Once you've stitched over the whole design, carefully tear away the tissue paper, leaving the tacking on the fabric. (you can also buy water soluble paper to help in this stage). If you're working on a light or delicate fabric, then be very very careful when removing the paper so you don't damage the fabric. The tacking stitch outline can be removed as you progress, or after the embroidery is completed.

My favourite way is to print the design in reverse using my laser printer. Then I use heat to transfer the design to my fabric. I have an old heat press that is great for this as it applies the heat evenly and the press holds everything in place securely. This method only works for cotton and linen fabrics though as I have found that for the best results the transfer time needs to be in excess of 40 seconds and it requires a temperature of 195 degrees, so there is always a danger of scorching.

I don't know if this would be possible with an iron and would hesitate to recommend this method - but if you have access to a heat press and laser printer then you could experiment - once you've found the ideal settings it's a great method as even the tiniest details can be transferred without difficulty.

If you have successfully used another method, or have any hints you'd like to share then please do let me know so I can pass them on to Bustle & Sew readers. Meanwhile … happy stitching!

And finally ... time to put your feet up with a nice cup of tea (and a biscuit or three!)

November's bite-sized tips and trivia...

Speedy Stitching

Sewing machines were first purchased by the general public in the 1860s, often by women, which cut down their sewing time from approximately 14.5 hours by hand, to 1 hour using the machine and by 1863, the Singer Manufacturing Company were selling 20,000 machines a year for home use.

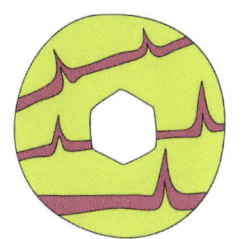

A Match made in Heaven

When making a garment from plaid fabric you need to add at least a quarter to your total yardage to allow for pattern matching.

Sweet dreams

Feeling less than creative? Allow yourself time and space to sit and dream, let your imagination run free and give your ideas your full attention. Daydreaming isn't a waste of time, it's food for the creative soul.

The Key to Success

Use dots of different coloured nail varnish to identify your keys. Far cheaper than having different-coloured keys cut.

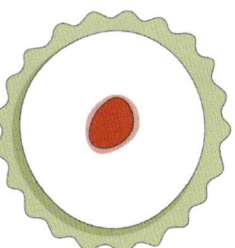

Hopping Mad!

Kangaroos use their tails for balance, so if you lift a kangaroo's tail off the ground it can't hop!

Carrots used to be Purple

The modern-day carrot wasn't cultivated until the sixteenth century when Dutch growers took mutant strains of the existing purple carrots including yellow and white and developed them into today's bright orange juicy vegetables. Before this pretty much all carrots were purple, and the rare yellow and white ones weren't encouraged as they were typically thin and not very tasty.

If you're reading this and looking forward to making some new projects, then you're unlikely to suffer from

ENETOPHOBIA

or a fear of pins

Causing a Stir

Stir-up Sunday falls on 23 November this year, so find your spoons, don your aprons and get stirring!

Conversion Tables

Volume

Imperial	Metric
2 fl oz	55 ml
3 fl oz	75 ml
5 fl oz (¼ pint)	150 ml
10 fl oz (½ pint)	275 ml
1 pint	570 ml
1 ¼ pint	725 ml
1 ¾ pint	1 litre
2 pint	1.2 litre
2½ pint	1.5 litre
4 pint	2.25 litres

Weights

Imperial	Metric
½ oz	10 g
¾ oz	20 g
1 oz	25 g
1½ oz	40 g
2 oz	50 g
2½ oz	60 g
3 oz	75 g
4 oz	110 g
4½ oz	125 g
5 oz	150 g
6 oz	175 g
7 oz	200 g
8 oz	225 g
9 oz	250 g
10 oz	275 g
12 oz	350 g
1 lb	450 g

Oven Temperatures

Gas Mark	°F	°C
1	275°F	140°C
2	300°F	150°C
3	325°F	170°C
4	350°F	180°C
5	375°F	190°C
6	400°F	200°C
7	425°F	220°C
8	450°F	230°C
9	475°F	240°C

American Cup Conversions

American	Imperial	Metric
1 cup flour	5oz	150g
1 cup caster/granulated sugar	8oz	225g
1 cup brown sugar	6oz	175g
1 cup butter/margarine/lard	8oz	225g
1 cup sultanas/raisins	7oz	200g
1 cup currants	5oz	150g
1 cup ground almonds	4oz	110g
1 cup golden syrup	12oz	350g
1 cup uncooked rice	7oz	200g
1 cup grated cheese	4oz	110g
1 stick butter	4oz	110g

Liquid Conversions

Imperial	Metric	American
½ fl oz	15 ml	1 tbsp
1 fl oz	30 ml	1/8 cup
2 fl oz	60 ml	¼ cup
4 fl oz	120 ml	½ cup
8 fl oz	240 ml	1 cup
16 fl oz	480 ml	1 pint

Note: A pint isn't always a pint: in British, Australian and often Canadian recipes you'll see an imperial pint listed as 20 fluid ounces. American and some Canadian recipes use the the American pint measurement, which is 16 fluid ounces.

Movember Hoops

Templates are actual size and reversed for tracing onto the paper sie of your Bonadaweb

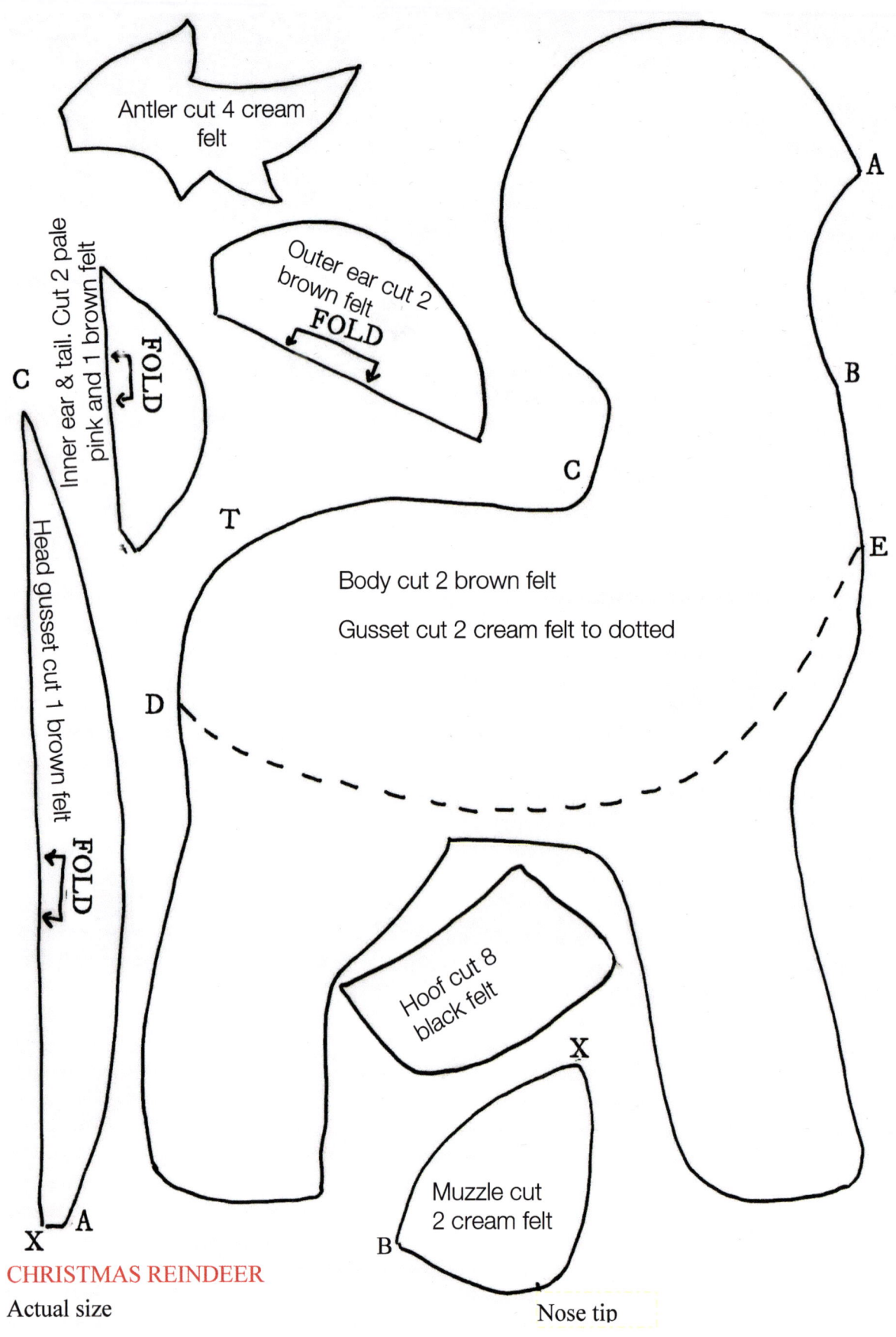

TRUE FRIENDS HOOP ART

Actual size. Use the reversed template for tracing the applique shapes onto the paper side of your Bondaweb.

FLORAL ALPHABET
Actual size used for bookends

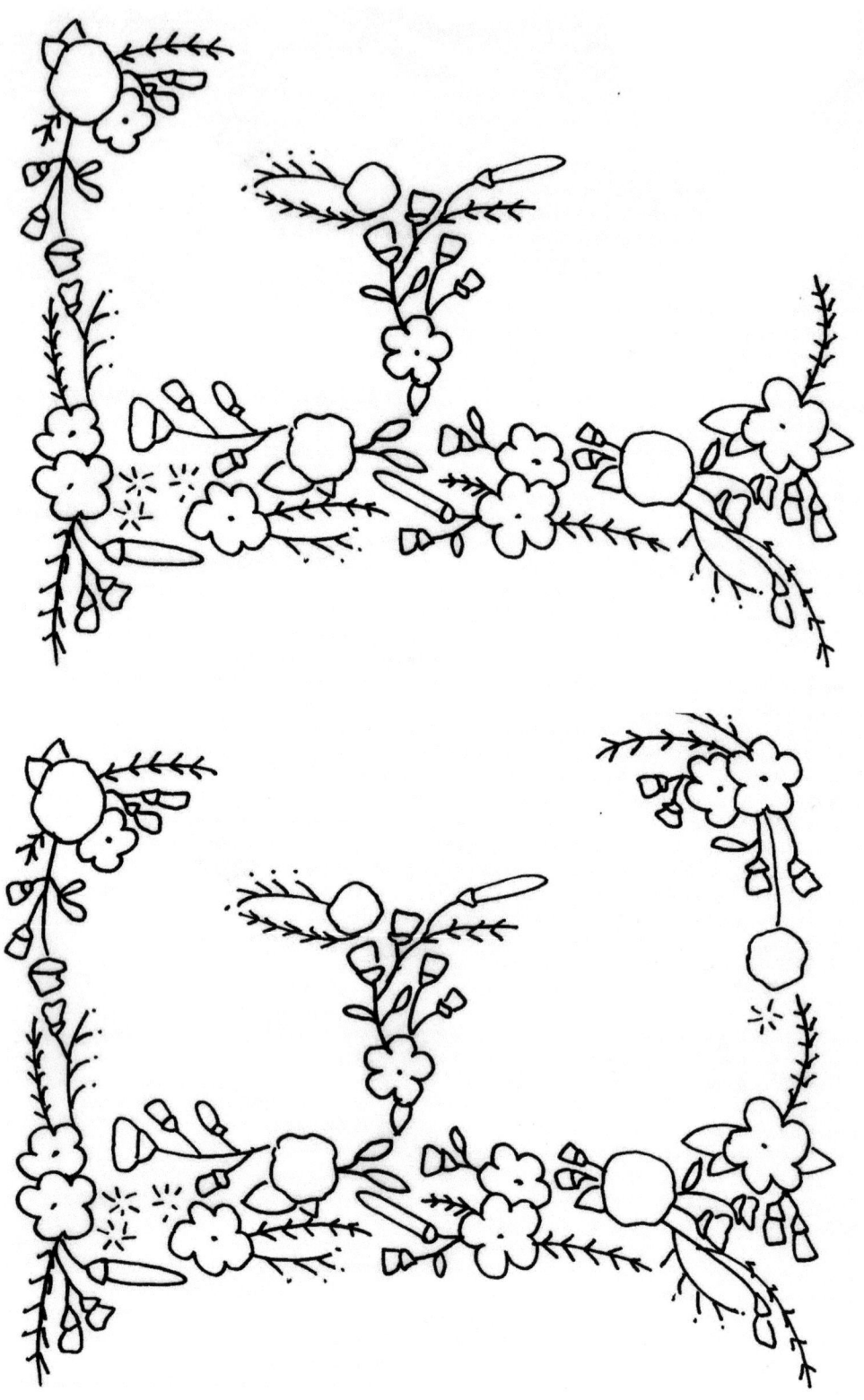

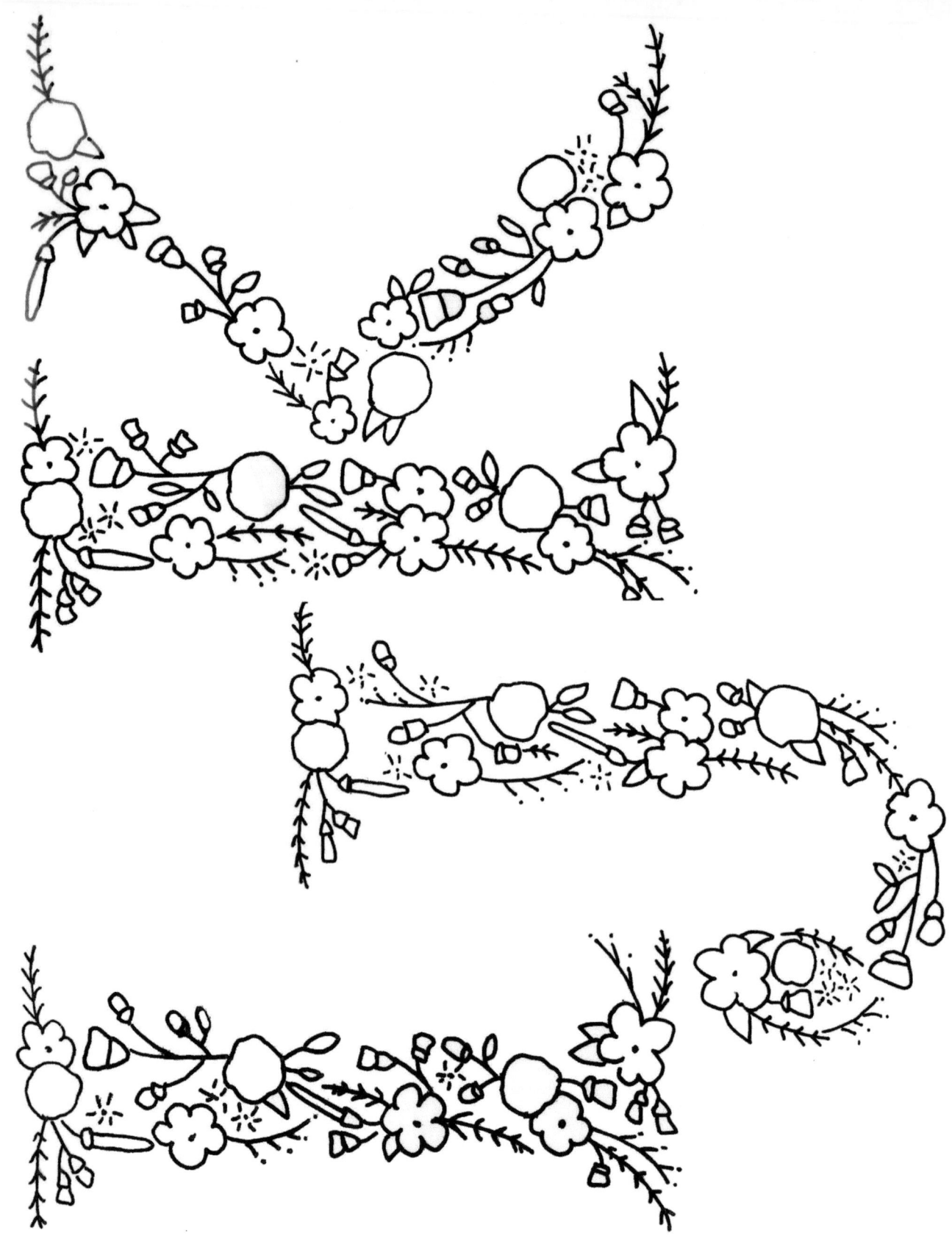

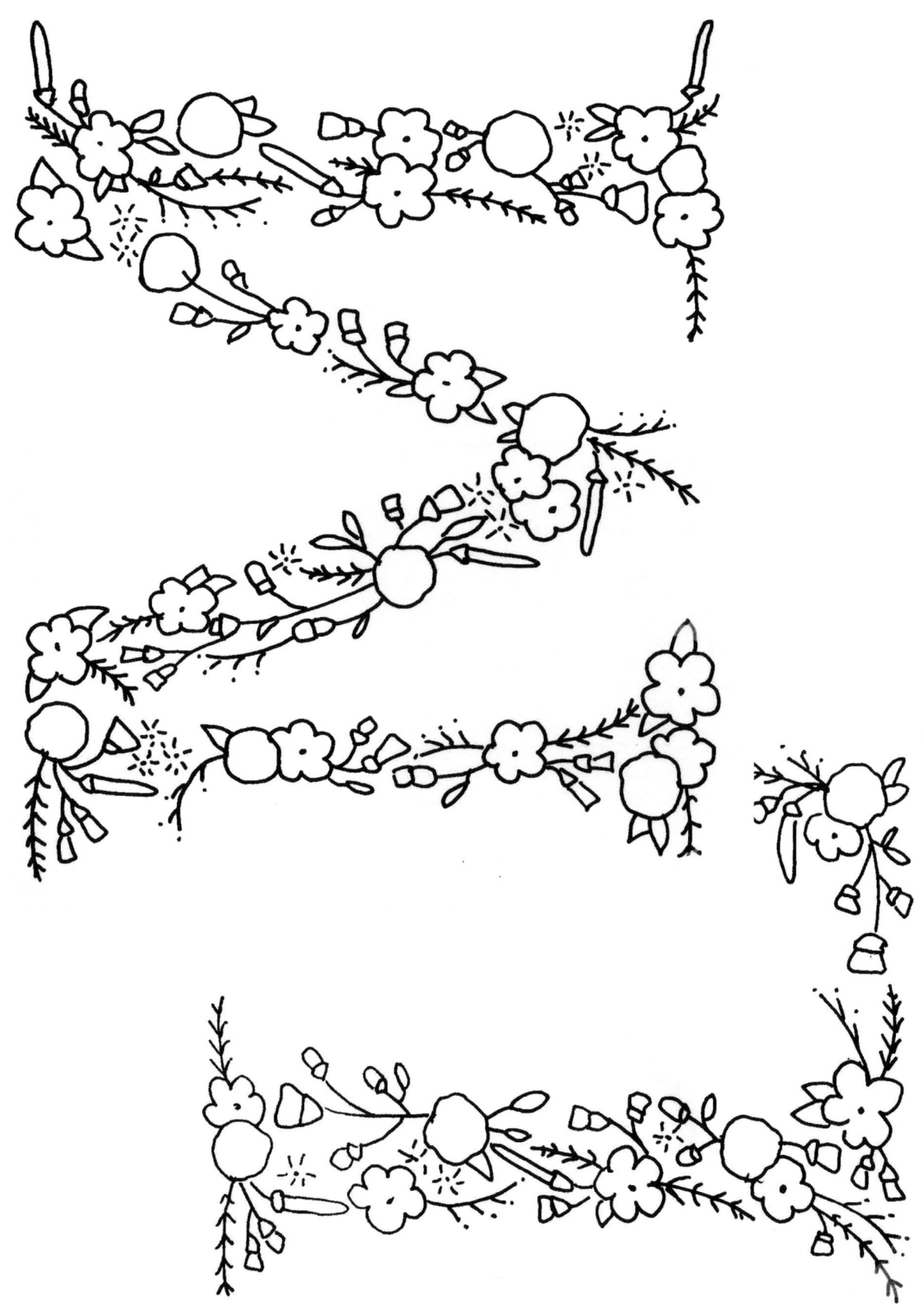

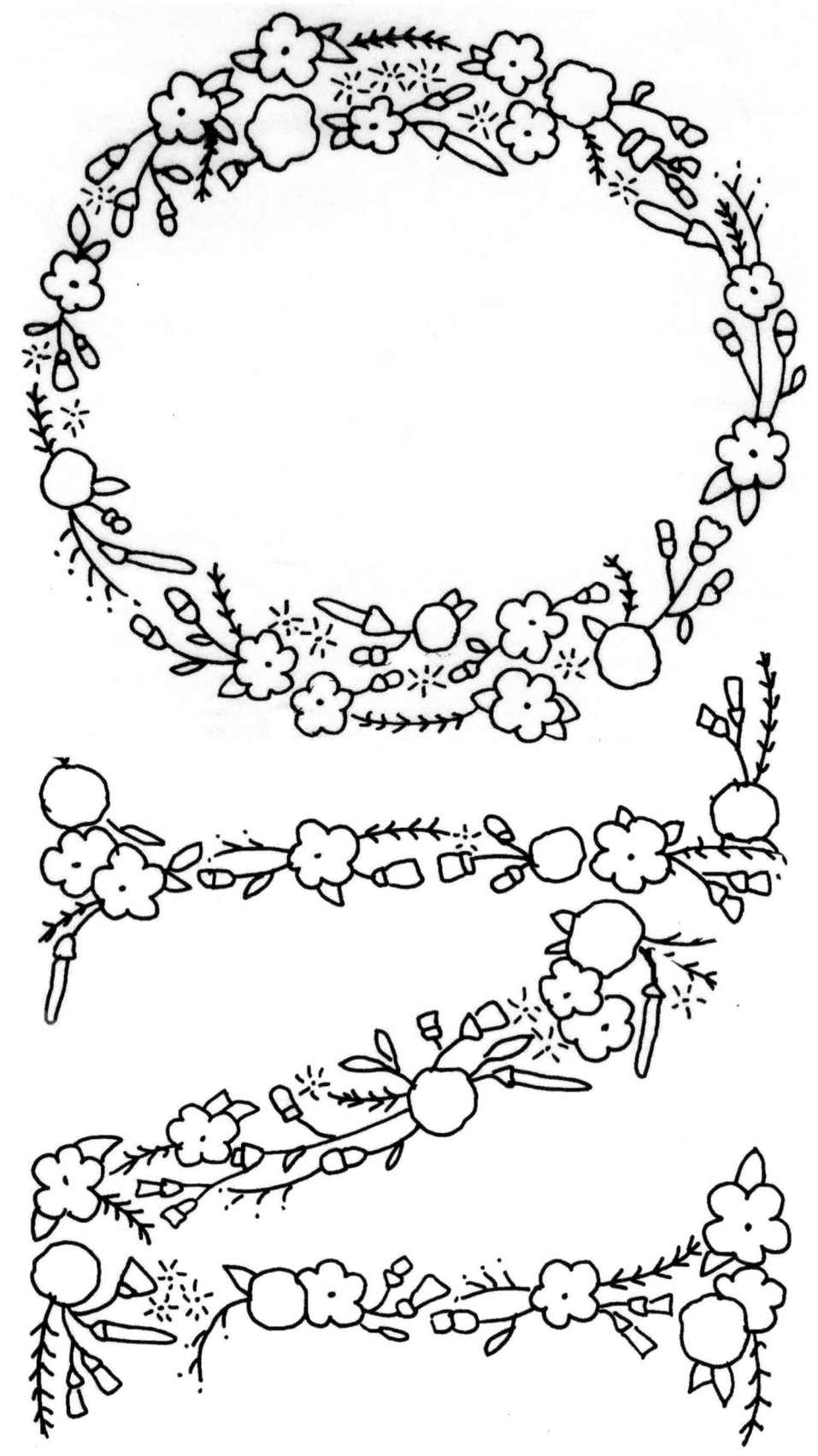

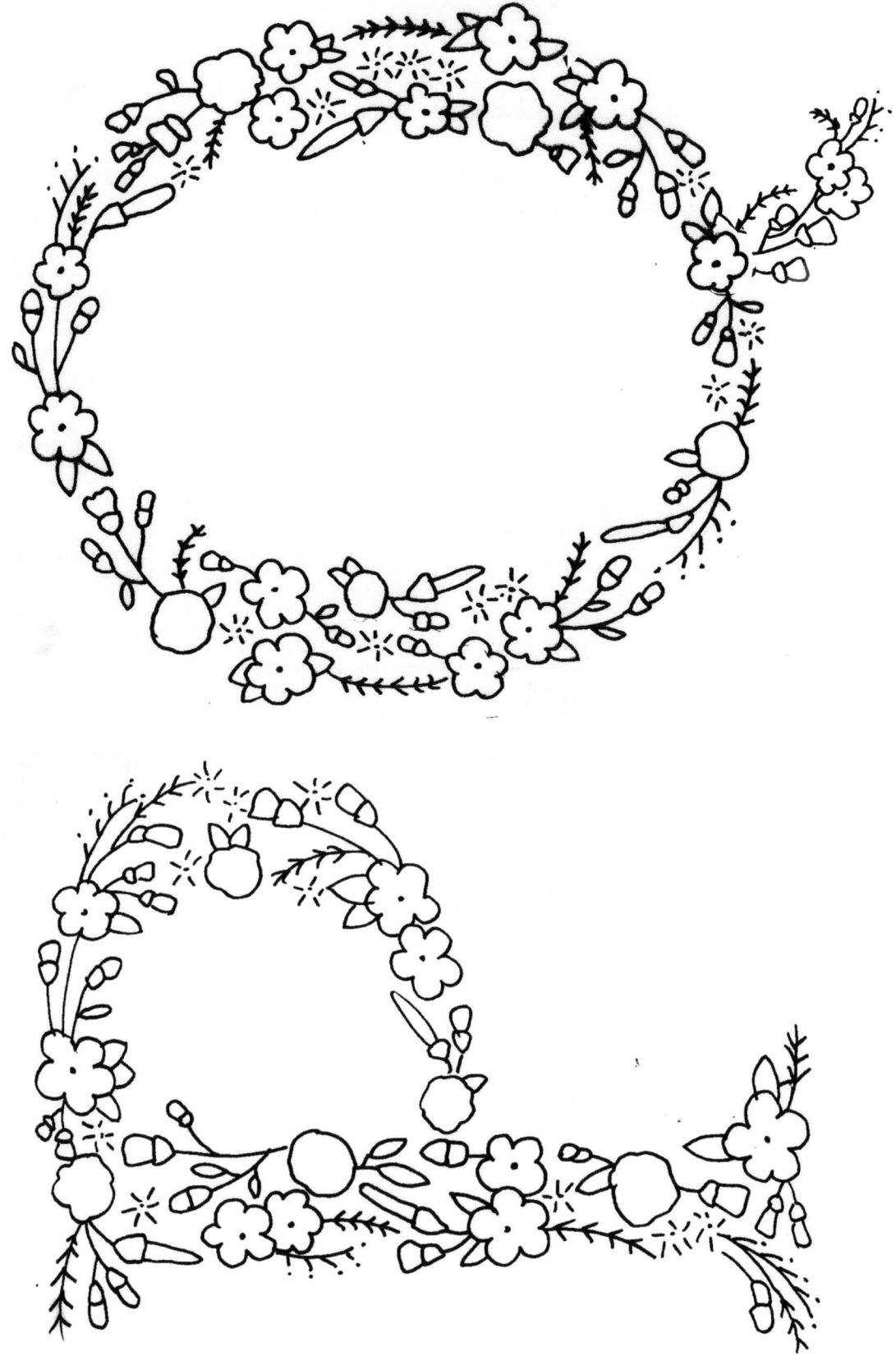

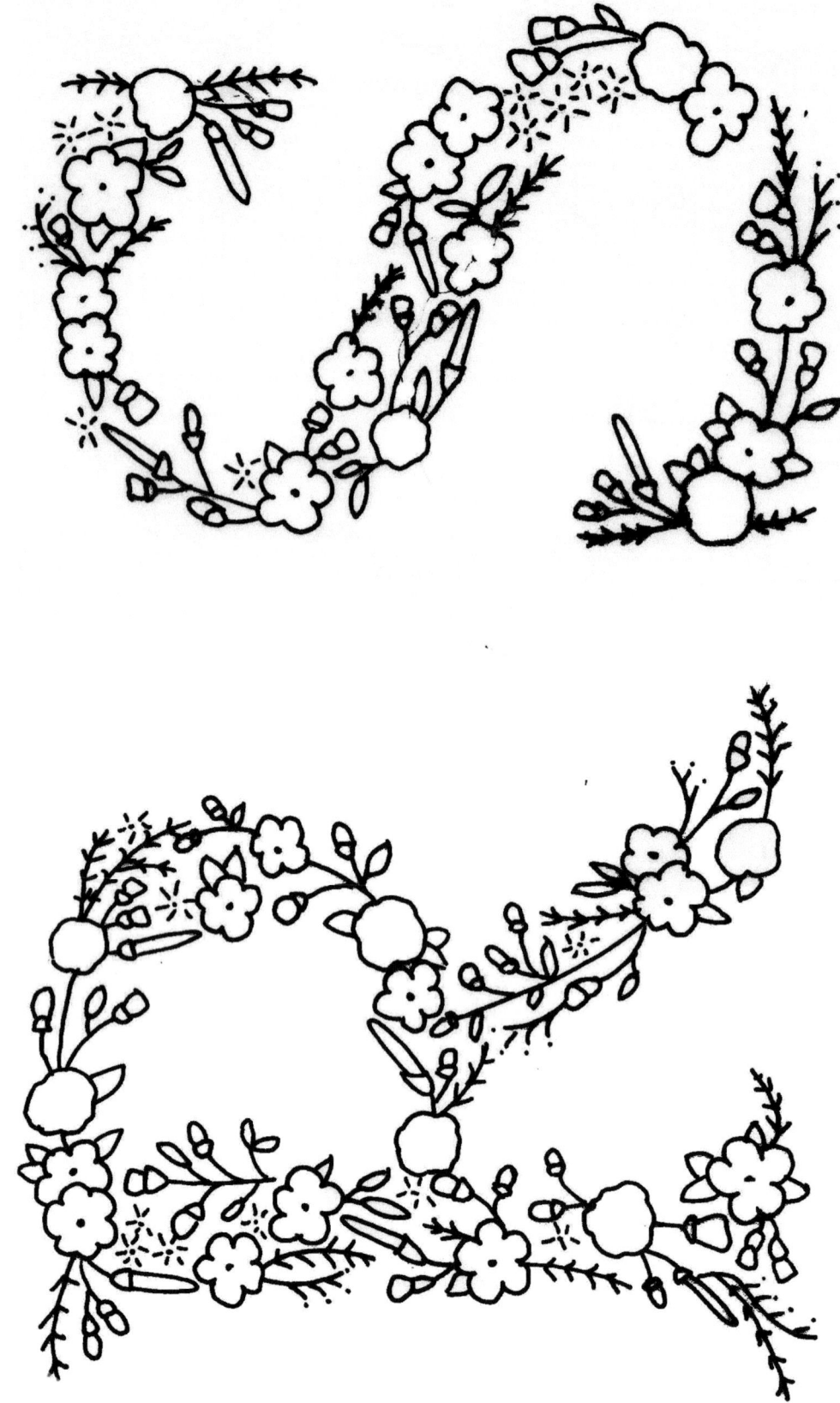

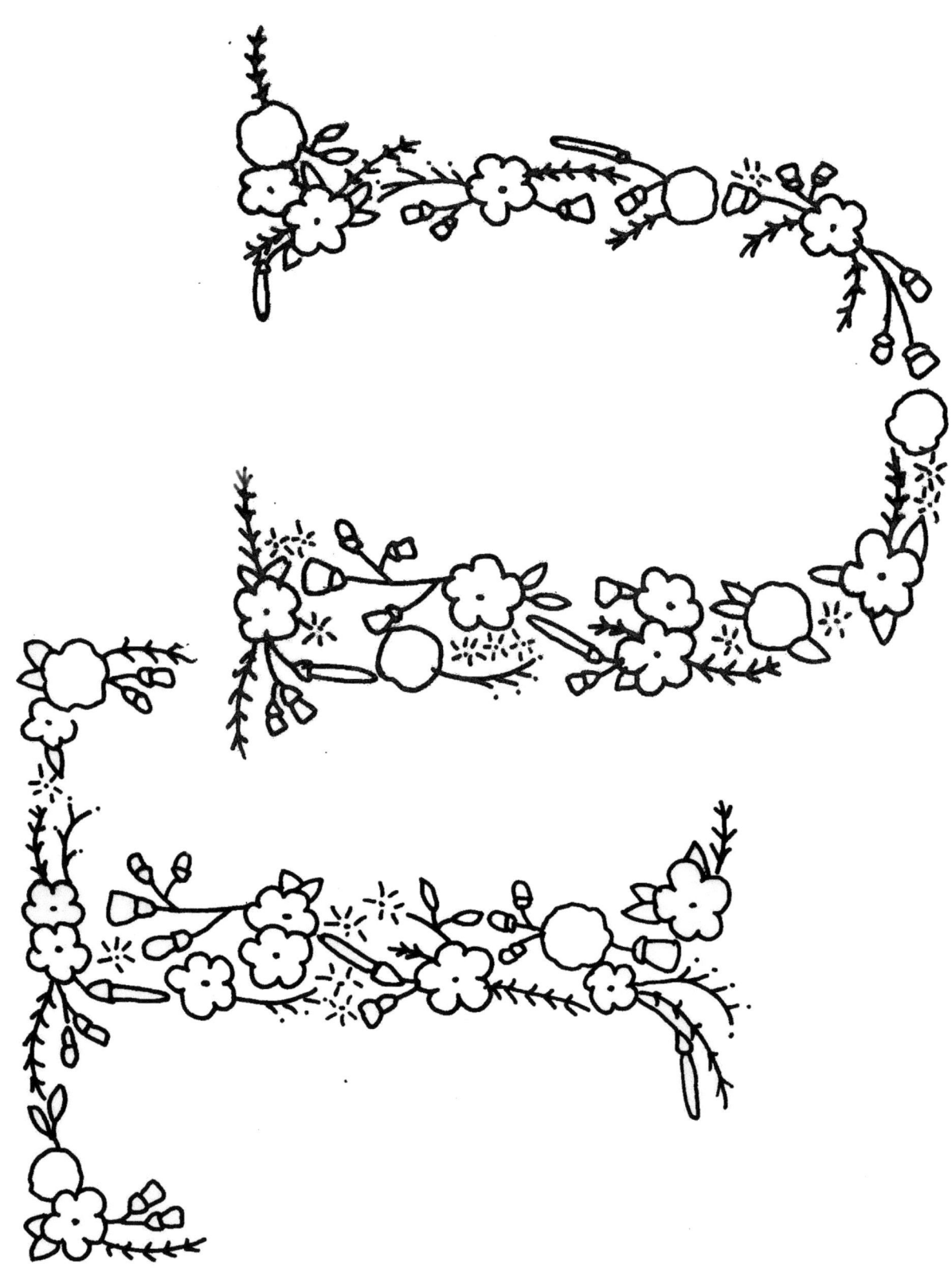

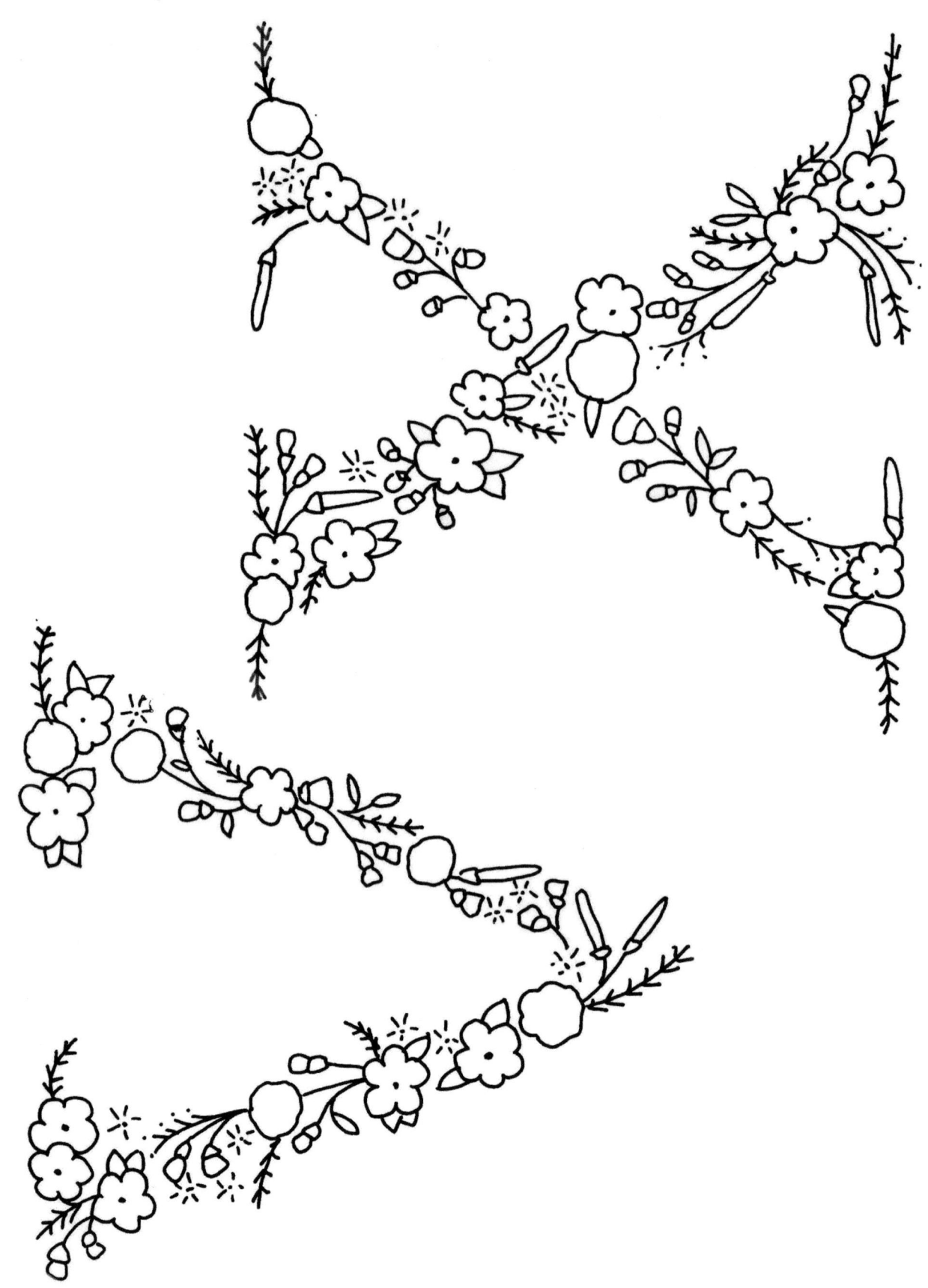

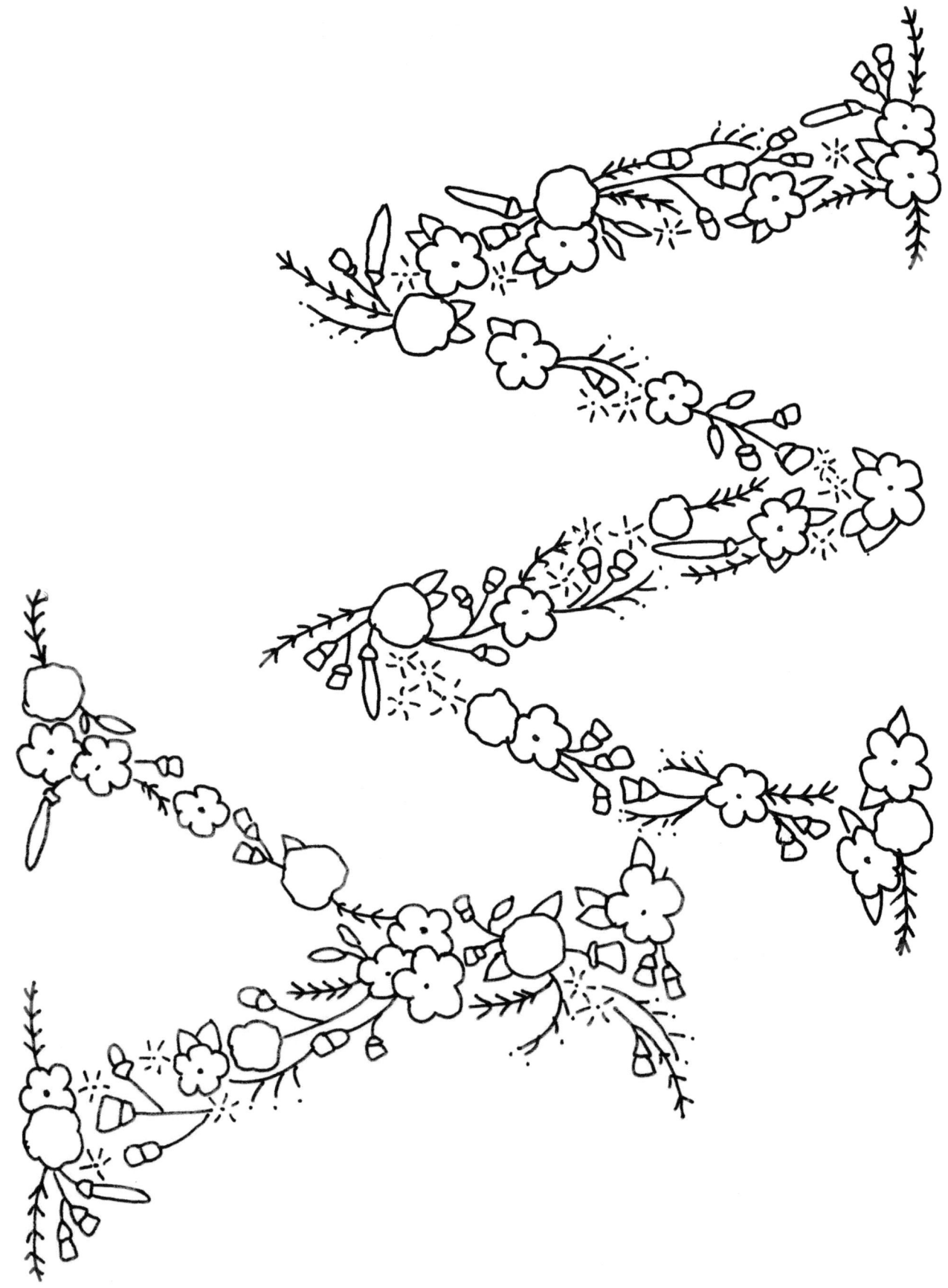

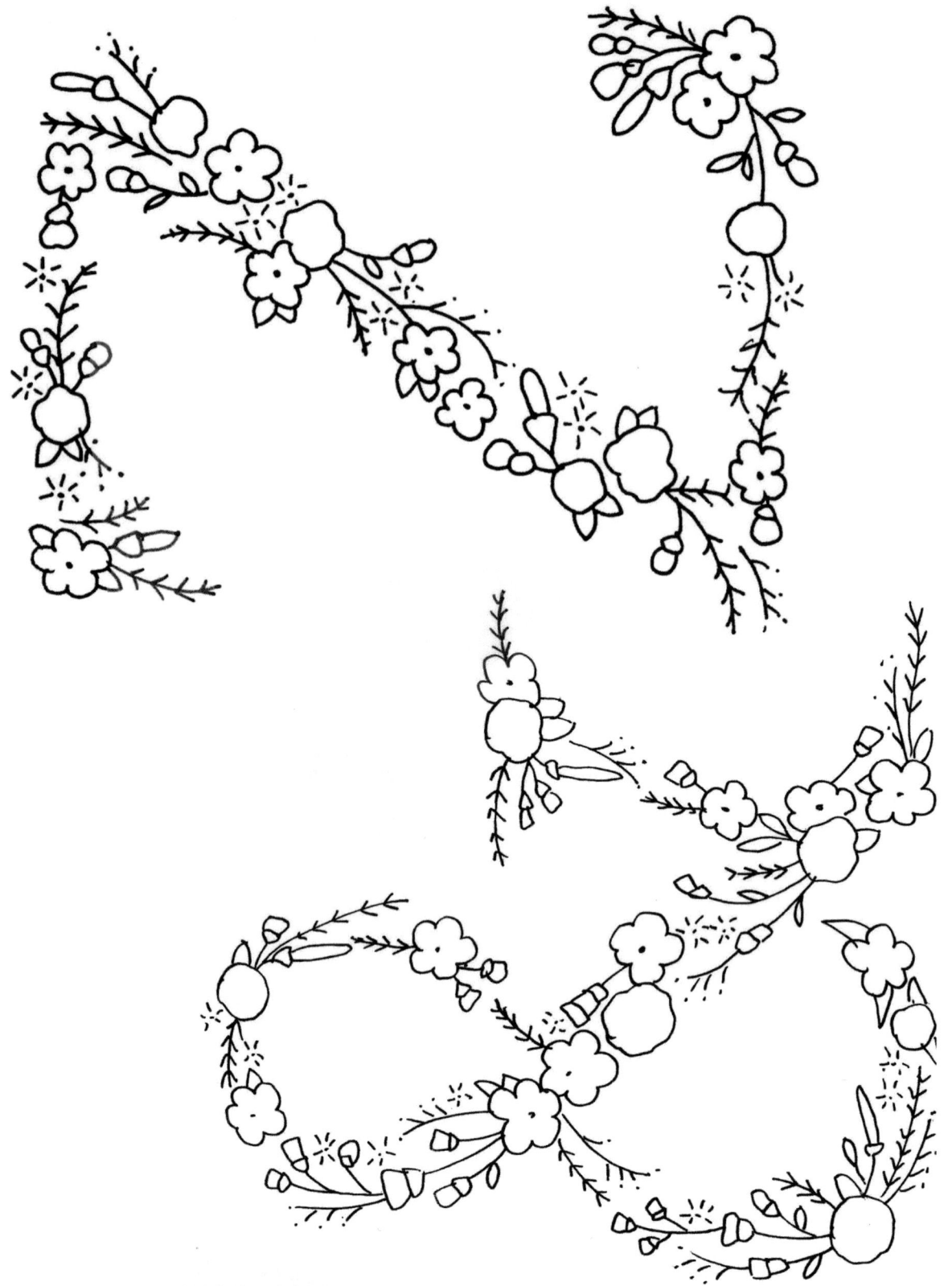

Candy Cone Mouse
Actual size.

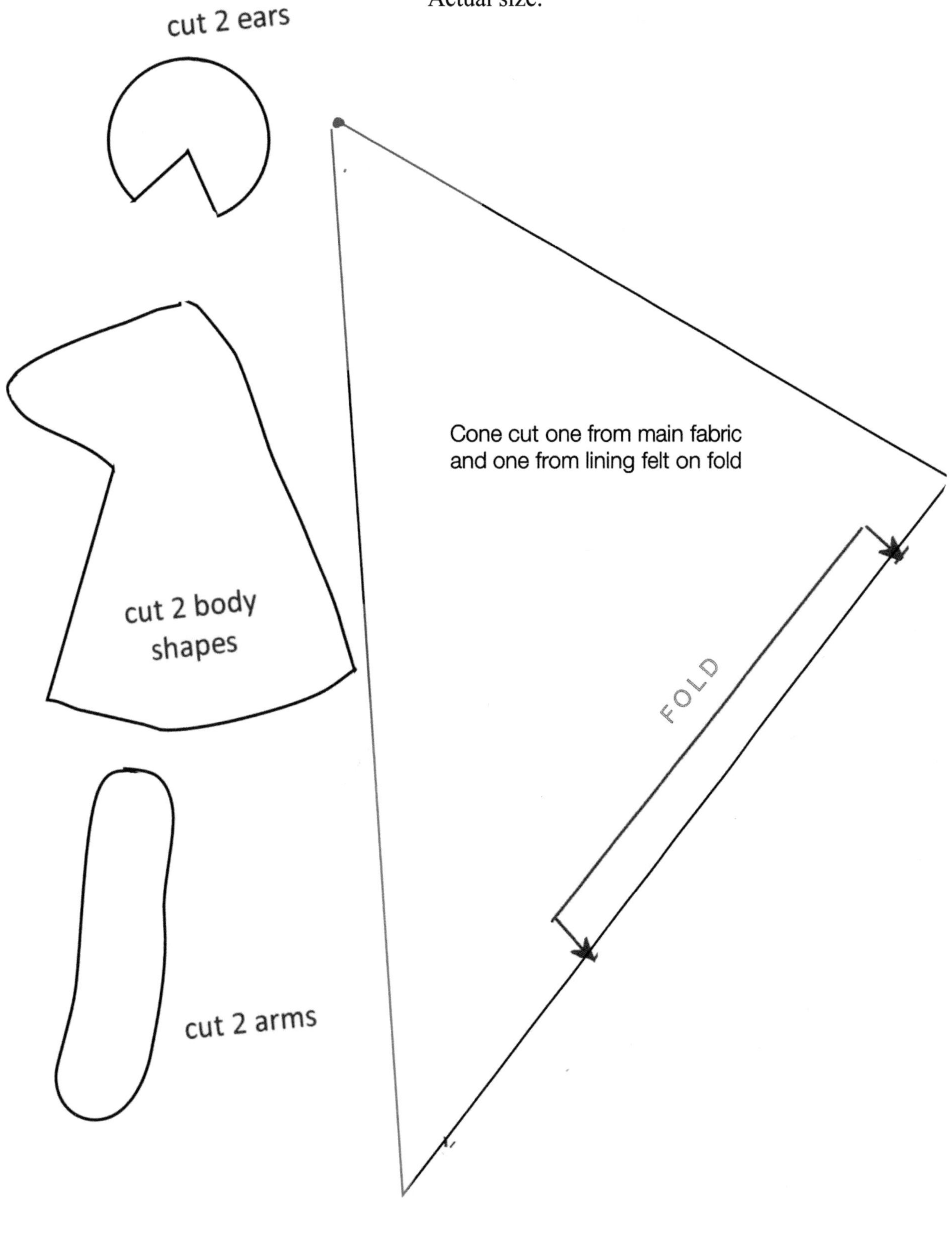

cut 2 ears

cut 2 body shapes

Cone cut one from main fabric and one from lining felt on fold

FOLD

cut 2 arms

Village Applique Shade

Actual size and reversed for tracing onto the paper side of your Bondaweb.

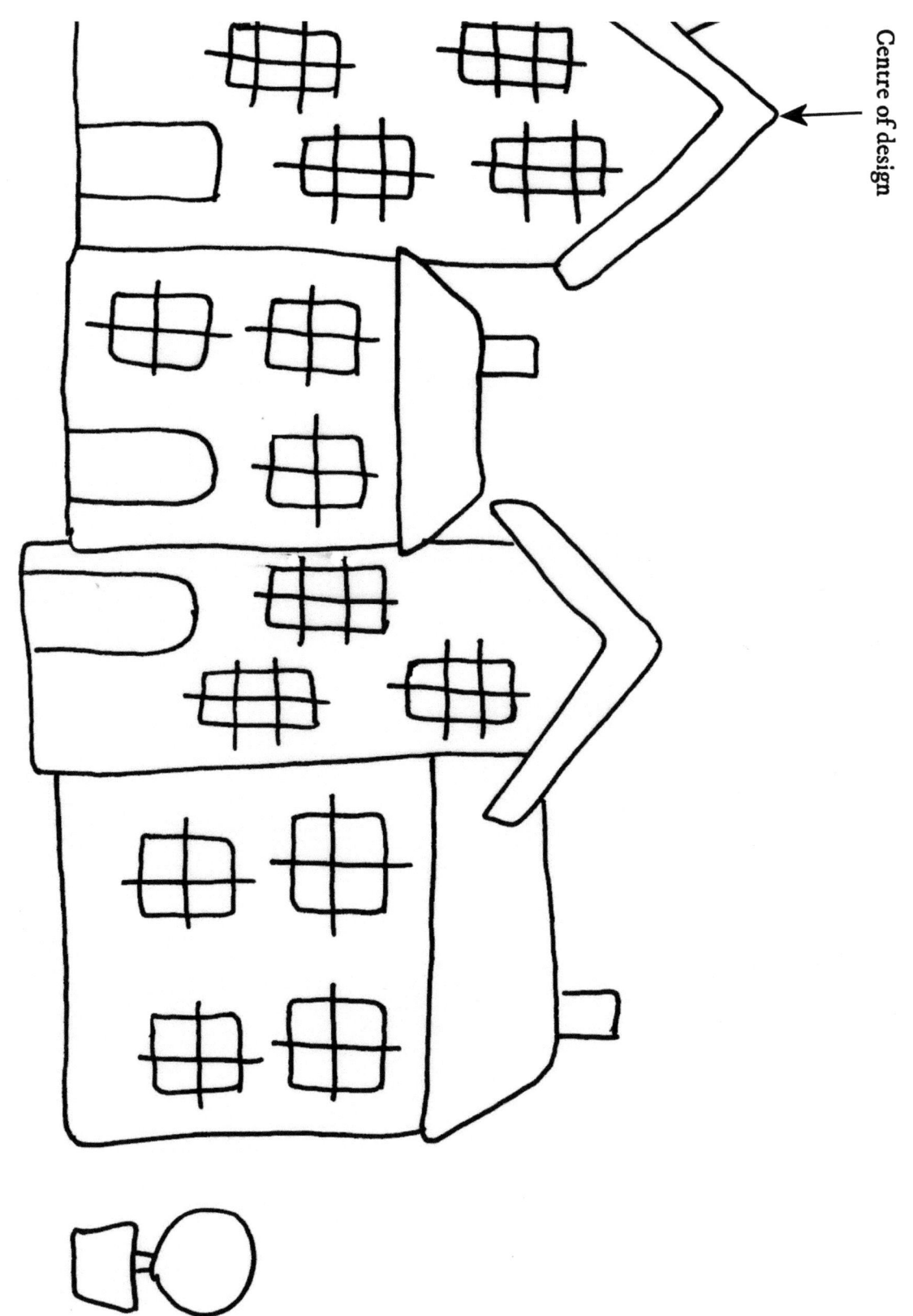

Printed in Great Britain
by Amazon.co.uk, Ltd.,
Marston Gate.